The Arapaho
and Their History

By Natalie M. Rosinsky

Content Adviser: Bruce Bernstein, Ph.D.,
Assistant Director for Cultural Resources,
National Museum of the American Indian, Smithsonian Institution

Reading Adviser: Rosemary G. Palmer, Ph.D.,
Department of Literacy, College of Education,
Boise State University

COMPASS POINT BOOKS
MINNEAPOLIS, MINNESOTA

Compass Point Books
3109 West 50th Street, #115
Minneapolis, MN 55410

Visit Compass Point Books on the Internet at *www.compasspointbooks.com*
or e-mail your request to *custserv@compasspointbooks.com*

On the cover: An 1861 painting of an Arapaho and Cheyenne encampment by Ester Yates Frazier

Photographs ©: Courtesy, Colorado Historical Society, cover, 4, 21; Prints Old & Rare, back
cover (far left); Library of Congress, back cover, 15, 25; MPI/Getty Images, 5, 14, 23, 28; North
Wind Picture Archives, 6, 32; The Denver Public Library, 7, 20; John Elk III, 9; Smithsonian
American Art Museum, Washington, D.C./Art Resource, N.Y., 10; David Muench/Corbis, 12;
Layne Kennedy/Corbis, 13; Beloit College, Logan Museum of Anthropology, 16, 17; U.S.
National Archives & Records Administration, 18, 24, 31, 33; Marilyn "Angel" Wynn, 19, 34, 35,
37, 38, 39; Corbis, 22, 27; Werner Forman/Corbis, 26; Pictorial Parade/Getty Images, 30;
Raymond Bial, 40, 41; John Cross/The Free Press, 48.

Creative Director: Terri Foley
Managing Editor: Catherine Neitge
Art Director: Keith Griffin
Photo Researcher: Marcie C. Spence
Designer/Page production: Bradfordesign, Inc./Les Tranby
Cartographer: XNR Productions, Inc.
Educational Consultant: Diane Smolinski

Library of Congress Cataloging-in-Publication Data
Rosinsky, Natalie M. (Natalie Myra)
  The Arapaho and their history / by Natalie M. Rosinsky.
      p. cm—(We the people)
  Includes bibliographical references and index.
  ISBN 0-7565-0831-2 (hardcover)
  1. Arapaho Indians—History—Juvenile literature. 2. Arapaho Indians—Social life and customs—
Juvenile literature. I. Title. II. We the people (Series) (Compass Point Books)
E99.A7R67 2005
978.004'97354—dc22   2004018961

TABLE OF CONTENTS

"In Cold Blood" 4

Who Are the Arapaho? 8

Traveling Hunters 12

Family and Community 18

Beliefs and Ceremonies 22

Peace Leaders and War Leaders 26

"We Wish to Live" 28

Years of Change 31

The Arapaho Today 38

Glossary 42

Did You Know? 43

Important Dates 44

Important People 45

Want to Know More? 46

Index 48

IN COLD BLOOD

A white flag of truce guarded the combined Cheyenne and Arapaho campsite at Sand Creek, Colorado. An American flag hung alongside it on that crisp morning of November 29, 1864. President Abraham Lincoln had personally given this flag to Chief Black Kettle three years before. These flags, together with the peace talks Cheyenne Chiefs Black

U.S. soldiers ignore a flag of truce at the Sand Creek campsite.

Kettle and White Antelope had just completed with Colorado's governor, should have kept the people there safe. Yet, at dawn, more than 200 Cheyenne and Arapaho men, women, and children were massacred by U.S. soldiers.

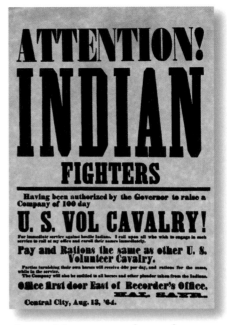

A recruiting poster seeks cavalry volunteers to fight Indians in Colorado.

The troops were led by Colonel John M. Chivington, who infamously defended the killing of innocent Indian children by saying, "Nits breed lice." Chivington's soldiers showed no mercy. Major Scott Anthony reported, "There was one little child, probably three years old, just big enough to walk through the sand … I saw one man get off his horse … and draw up his rifle and fire, he missed the child. Another man came up and said, 'Let me try. …' A third man came up … and the little fellow dropped." Other children were clubbed to

Cavalry soldiers charge into the Sand Creek camp.

death. Many were screaming with terror. Soldiers killed women and cut up their bodies. One pregnant woman was stabbed and her yet-to-be born baby ripped from her body. Another soldier remembered that he "did not see a body of a man, woman, child [that was not] scalped."

While the few warriors at the camp managed to kill eight of their attackers, White Antelope refused to go back on his word. He had promised to keep the peace. After shouting "Stop! Stop!" to the troops, White Antelope folded his arms in front of him and began to sing a

6

traditional death song: "Nothing lives long except the earth and the mountains." Soldiers slaughtered him.

In 1865, the U.S. Congress investigated this attack. It concluded that Colonel Chivington had deliberately planned and committed "a massacre." Chivington knew "their friendly character," yet he "surprised and murdered, in cold blood, the unsuspecting men, women, and children on Sand Creek … and then … boasted of the 'brave deeds.'" The government, however, never officially punished Chivington. Instead, it offered Black Kettle, who had survived, extra land in a treaty later that year as payment for what it called his "injuries."

This massacre was one terrible event among many changes that forever altered the lives of the Arapaho people.

An Arapaho girl was the only child to survive the Sand Creek Massacre.

WHO ARE THE ARAPAHO?

The Arapaho (pronounced uh-RAP-uh-ho) are a native people of the central Great Plains. Many historians believe that more than 10,000 years ago, ancestors of the Arapaho crossed a land bridge from Asia to North America and slowly spread eastward. At first, they lived between the upper Great Lakes and the northeast coast. We know this because the Arapaho speak one of the Algonquian languages that were common there.

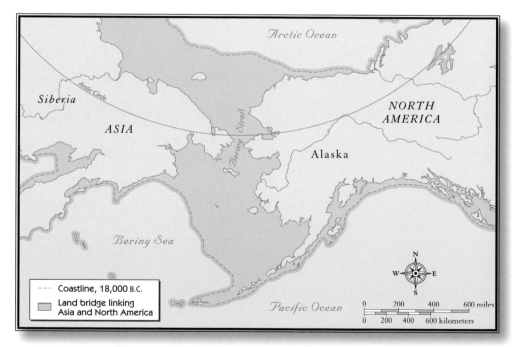

Thousands of years ago, a land bridge linked Asia and North America.

The Arapaho have long lived near the Wind River in Wyoming.

Sometime before 1700, ancestors of the Arapaho moved west. Along with other native peoples, they lived in a large territory between the Mississippi River and the Rocky Mountains. It included parts of what are now the states of Wyoming, Colorado, South Dakota, Nebraska, Kansas, Iowa, Missouri, and Oklahoma. Some Arapaho lived in the northern part of this region, while others lived in the southern part. The Cheyenne were a traditional ally of the Arapaho. Their enemies included the Comanche, Pawnee, Shoshone, and Ute.

Many tribes, including the Comanche, shared the vast Great Plains.

There were more than 30 different tribes on the Great Plains. Some spoke very different languages. To communicate, the tribes developed a wordless sign language that used hand signals.

In their own language, the Arapaho called themselves the Hinonoeino, which means "our people." Other tribes and, later, settlers called them the Arapaho. In the Pawnee language, this name sounds like the word for trader, tirapihu. The Arapaho did much trading. Their name also sounds like the Crow word Alappaho, which means "people with tattoos." The Arapaho tattooed small circles on themselves. The Arapaho people have officially adopted "Arapaho" as their tribal name.

Today, there are more than 7,000 Arapaho. About 2,500 Northern Arapaho live on or near the Wind River

Reservation in Wyoming. They share this land with the Shoshone tribe. About 4,500 Southern Arapaho share a reservation with the Cheyenne in western Oklahoma. These reservations are much smaller than the Plains where the Arapaho once lived.

Most Arapaho today live in Wyoming and Oklahoma.

TRAVELING HUNTERS

The Great Plains include rock-filled and flat, grassy areas with few sources of water. Few plants other than grass grow during the hot, dry summers, and virtually none grow in the long, cold winters. To survive, the Arapaho hunted for food. These nomads did not have permanent homes. Instead, they moved frequently to find and follow food.

Prairie grass covered the Great Plains.

The buffalo provided the Arapaho with food and other necessities.

Buffalo was their main food. The Arapaho used the whole animal, so large herds of buffalo provided the Arapaho with shelter, tools, and clothing. The Arapaho even used buffalo hooves to make special rattles. There were so many buffalo that, as one 19th century scientist later said, "It would have been as easy to count … the number of leaves in a forest as to calculate the number of buffaloes living at any given time previous to 1870."

When the Arapaho first lived on the Plains, men hunted buffalo on foot. Sometimes, these hunters wore buffalo skins to sneak up on the animals. At other times, hunters might wear wolf skins. The smell of this enemy helped hunters to frighten the buffalo off cliffs or trick them into narrow, fenced-in canyons. Hunters killed buffalo with spears.

Hunting buffalo became easier after Spanish explorers and settlers brought horses to the Plains. Arapaho men

Native Americans on horseback pursue a herd of buffalo.

traded or raided others for horses. By 1730, Arapaho men hunted on horseback. Using bows and arrows and moving quickly, they were able to kill more buffalo. A horse pulled the heavy load of slaughtered dead buffalo on a travois back to their campsite. The camp was located near water, if any was close, since water is heavy to carry. A good campsite also had enough grass to feed the horses.

A 1908 photo by Edward S. Curtis shows a woman scraping a hide.

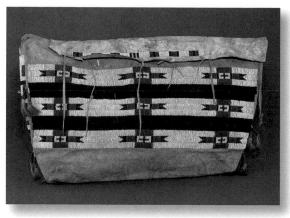

A beaded Arapaho "possible bag" could carry every possible thing.

Arapaho women prepared and cooked buffalo meat and other foods. Some meat was eaten right away, but some was dried for winter use. Elk, deer, and antelope were other important foods. Women also gathered wild fruits and vegetables when they were available. Sometimes, they mixed dried meat and fruit with buffalo fat into a food called pemmican. Women also prepared buffalo and other animal hides used for shelter, tools, and clothing. They stored foods and other belongings in hide sacks called parfleches. Other tools included bone needles and animal sinews, which women used to sew clothing.

Arapaho lived in cone-shaped, temporary dwellings called tipis. For each tipi, 15 to 20 buffalo hides were sewn together and stretched across a circular bundle of poles.

Often, tipis had an inner hide lining decorated with drawings. An open space at the top of the tipi let smoke escape from the campfire inside. Tipis could be taken apart quickly when it was time to move. Inside the tipi, Arapaho slept on buffalo hides.

A special 1885 Arapaho dance dress had painted leather and many feathers.

Men wore animal skin leggings, shirts, and breechcloths. Women wore long, fringed dresses and leggings made of animal skin. Often, they enjoyed decorating special clothing with dyed porcupine quills or beads. The Arapaho protected their feet in soft leather moccasins with tougher, rawhide soles. In winter, heavy buffalo robes kept the Arapaho warm.

17

FAMILY AND COMMUNITY

A large family lived in an Arapaho tipi. Besides the mother, father, and unmarried children, the grandparents and other older relatives often lived there as well. A mother's family was important because women owned tipis and their contents. It was also the Arapaho custom for newly married couples to live in a tipi next to the wife's mother.

Buffalo meat dries in front of an Arapaho tipi in 1870.

Girls learned skills by watching and helping female relatives. Playing with small dolls and tipis was another way to practice being a mother. To become good hunters and warriors, boys ran, swam, and played with bows and arrows. They enjoyed a hoop and stick game. It took a good eye to get that stick through the tiny rolling hoop. Ball

Arapaho women, a child, and a baby in a cradleboard pose in a 19th-century photo.

and stick games were popular with adults as well as children. Older relatives told stories that taught children about Arapaho customs and beliefs. Often, these tales involved creatures such as Spider who learned from making foolish mistakes. Some tales were about heroes, such as the first Arapaho to kill a buffalo.

This Arapaho man, who posed for a photo in the early 1900s, was named Goes in the Lodge.

The Arapaho had another, important way of passing along traditions. This was membership in groups called lodges that had their own special knowledge and ceremonies. Starting from the age of 12, Arapaho boys and men belonged to one of seven lodges. The first lodge a boy could join was the Kit Fox Society. Later, he might become a member of the Blackbird or Wild Rosebush Lodge. As Arapaho men grew older, they too joined different lodges and gained other knowledge. Girls and women belonged to the Buffalo Lodge. Sometimes, the best sewers also joined a lodge for decorating with quills and beads.

In the winter, when finding food was hardest, the Arapaho traveled in small bands of several families. This

*An 1861 oil painting shows an Arapaho and Cheyenne encampment
in what is now downtown Denver, Colorado.*

kept people from hunting the same animals. In other
seasons, they traveled in larger bands. Men traded extra
meat with other tribes for different foods or items. During
the summer, bands gathered together as a tribe. The
Arapaho visited and held their most sacred ceremony, the
Sun Dance, then. It was a tradition among some
neighboring Plains peoples, too.

BELIEFS AND CEREMONIES

The Sun Dance Ceremony lasted between four and eight days. For this summer event, the Arapaho built a special camp with a sacred, central pole. At its top, they placed objects they considered holy. Arapaho taking part in the ceremony first made themselves pure. To do this, they spent time in a sweat lodge and did not eat. Then, through special songs, dances, and shorter ceremonies, they

Plains Indians conduct a Sun Dance ceremony in Oklahoma.

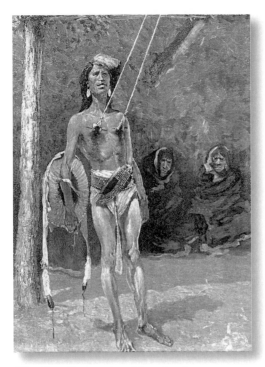

The Sun Dance ritual involved painful piercings.

honored the spirits and renewed their connection to them.

The Arapaho believed that willingly experiencing pain was an important way to honor the spirits. It was a way to thank them and become more holy. To do this, an Arapaho man might take part in the main Sun Dance ritual. This involved piercing his chest or back with pieces of wood attached to a rope. This rope hung from the top of the sacred pole. A Sun Dancer then stood and danced until his movements tore the wood pieces from his body. His blood and pain were a religious sacrifice.

Lodge leaders had some of the special knowledge needed to perform such ceremonies correctly. The

*The medicine bag of Little Big Mouth is visible behind his
tipi in this 1900 photo taken near Fort Sill, Oklahoma.*

medicine man also supposedly had special knowledge of
the spirit world. This respected leader helped Arapaho
people choose items for their own medicine bags. Arapaho
believed these things kept them safe. A medicine bag

represented a person's special relationship with one of the world's many spirits. An Arapaho person discovered this relationship in a dream or a vision.

An Arapaho man smokes the pipe in this Edward S. Curtis photo.

The Arapaho also believed that one great spirit had created the world. They said that this spirit had given them their most sacred object, the Flat Pipe. It was an honor and a huge responsibility to carry this stone pipe, keep it safe, and smoke tobacco in it. Its protectors traveled only on foot. At night, they slept with the pipe in a special, large tent at the center of the Arapaho camp.

The Arapaho believed their ceremonies and traditions helped them pass through the four stages of life. After childhood and youth, they hoped to become responsible adults and then wise, older people.

25

PEACE LEADERS AND WAR LEADERS

In peaceful times, lodge leaders and other elders advised the tribe's chief. The Arapaho respected and obeyed this man because of skills he had shown. A chief was a successful hunter, trader, and diplomat. He spoke for his people when they met another tribe. He also settled any arguments among people within his tribe.

In wartime, the Arapaho selected another chief to lead them. They chose this war chief for his bravery and skills as a warrior. The Arapaho fought other tribes for

The headdress of Yellow Calf, an Arapaho chief

26

horses and, sometimes, for territory. In these raids, it was not always necessary to kill one's enemy. The Arapaho and neighboring tribes believed that touching an enemy with a hand or weapon or taking his horse was also a victory. This tradition was known as "counting coup" on the enemy. Warriors sometimes carried coup sticks that showed the number of enemies they had defeated in this way.

Chief Powder Face wears his war costume in the late 1860s.

When white settlers reached the Great Plains, though, war became more deadly. Even peaceful times brought terrible problems for the Arapaho and other tribes.

"WE WISH TO LIVE"

In 1803 , the United States bought a vast amount of land from France. This Louisiana Purchase included the Great Plains. Explorers Merriweather Lewis and William Clark

Lewis and Clark explored the Great Plains and lands to the west.

were sent by the U.S. government to map this area. Traders and, later, settlers and miners followed. The Arapaho way of life changed.

Native peoples had no immunity to diseases carried by traders and settlers, and many Arapaho died. Some Arapaho suffered by drinking the alcohol traders offered. In the 1840s, settlers began to travel through Arapaho territory on their way to Oregon. More settlers followed in 1848, after the United States won its war with Mexico and opened more land to settlement. When gold was discovered in California, miners came through Arapaho lands.

All these people changed the paths of the buffalo herds. The Arapaho began to lose their most important resource. As Chief Medicine Man later told government officials, "The buffalo were plenty, and made the prairie look black all around us. Now none are to be seen. … Our old people and little children are hungry for many days. … We wish to live."

Settlers travel through Wyoming on their way west in this 1865 W.H. Jackson painting.

In 1851, the Arapaho signed a treaty with the United States. The Arapaho gave up some land for the government's promise to keep homesteaders off remaining Arapaho territory. The United States broke this promise. Towns and mining camps sprang up on Arapaho land, which further separated Northern and Southern Arapaho from each other.

30

YEARS OF CHANGE

The Sand Creek Massacre of 1864 occurred during this time of increasing white settlement. Arapaho Chief Little Raven said after Sand Creek's few survivors reached his camp, "The massacre was too bad to stand." The Arapaho and Cheyenne united to fight against soldiers and settlers.

Little Raven

Chief Little Raven worked to get government land for his people and their allies. He succeeded. In 1867, the Arapaho and other Plains Indians signed the Treaty of Medicine Lodge, which created a reservation for the Southern Arapaho and Cheyenne in Oklahoma.

New railroads crossing the Plains brought more settlers and hunters. Buffalo grew even scarcer. Even

31

Passengers and crew shoot buffalo from the train as it heads through the West.

though they had signed further treaties, Northern Arapaho in Wyoming went hungry. Arapaho leaders helped their people then by having some warriors work as scouts for the U.S. Army. They earned money and supplies that they shared with their tribe.

The Northern Arapaho did not want to leave their traditional territory. Chiefs Medicine Man, Black Coal, and Sharp Nose worked to get northern land set aside for their people. In 1877, Black Coal and Sharp Nose traveled to

Washington, D.C., to meet with President Rutherford B. Hayes. Black Coal spoke for his people, saying "Our tribe held three councils before I came away and we all agreed that if you would give us good land—we are a small tribe—we will be happy. We would like to join the Snakes (Shoshone)."

Sharp Nose

Their trip was successful. By 1878, the Northern Arapaho were able to move to the Wyoming Wind River Reservation alongside the Shoshone people.

On their reservations, though, Arapaho continued to suffer losses. The government did not respect their traditions. Many children were forced to leave their families to learn white men's ways. These children attended faraway schools, where they were not allowed to speak their own language. Sometimes, even their names were changed. Some children ran away.

The Carlisle Industrial School for Indians in Pennsylvania was the first of these schools. One Arapaho girl described her life there. She explained, "We had to learn that clocks had something to do with the hours and

Students study in the library of the Carlisle Industrial School for Indians.

Arapaho women and children in 1870

minutes that the white people mentioned so often." This was different from her people's way of measuring time. She noted, "When the sun rose, when it was high in the sky, and when it set were all the divisions of the day that we had ever found necessary when we followed the old Arapaho road. When we went on the hunting trip or to a sun dance, we counted time by sleeps."

Yet some Arapaho, like artist Carl Sweezy, found that such Indian schools helped them make needed changes from what Sweezy called "the buffalo road" to the newer "corn road" facing native peoples. Chief Little Raven also thought it important that Arapaho children learn new ways as well as old.

In 1887, the United States passed the Dawes General Allotment Act. This law broke earlier treaties and took still more land away from the Southern Arapaho reservation. Unhappiness there increased.

Along with other native peoples, some Arapaho began to look for comfort in religion. They became involved in the Ghost Dance movement. This belief offered native peoples the hope of seeing their dead loved ones again. It promised a better life here on earth as well as after death. The government feared that Ghost Dancers would revolt, though, and outlawed this movement. Some Arapaho became involved in religious practices using a plant called

Wovoka, a Paiute prophet (seated), who revitalized the Ghost Dance movement, met with the Arapaho in Wyoming.

peyote, which gave them visions. These practices were later outlawed as well.

One religious tradition of the Arapaho was also banned for a time. Between 1904 and 1934, the Sun Dance ceremony was outlawed. As Carl Sweezy noted, the "Arapaho have always been a religious people." They again suffered because of this forced change in their way of life.

THE ARAPAHO TODAY

During the 20th century, the Arapaho worked to regain some rights. In 1935, the Southern Arapaho formed a constitutional government with their reservation neighbors, the Cheyenne. In 1947, Northern Arapaho tribal leaders got legal control of mineral rights on their reservation so the Arapaho, rather than outside companies, would benefit from mining done there.

Today, the Southern Arapaho elect a business council of four Arapaho and four Cheyenne. This council helps run government programs that aid people on the reservation. It manages the few oil wells there. The council also manages other tribal businesses, including

The Arapaho today keep their traditions alive.

Cattle graze on the Northern Arapaho's large ranch.

farming. Some people on the reservation need jobs, but others commute to jobs in nearby cities.

The Northern Arapaho also have an elected business council of six people. It follows the wishes of the Arapaho people on important matters, rather than a written constitution. This is a traditional Arapaho way of reaching agreements. The council represents its people in dealings with the Wyoming and federal governments.

The Northern Arapaho run a large cattle ranch on the reservation, but they need more jobs on and near this territory. Many Arapaho remain unemployed. They are

Two girls take part in a powwow at the Wind River Reservation.

also concerned about health care and want more laws to protect their land, air, and water.

In the 1970s, Northern Arapaho began to work to bring back their own language. Only a few older Arapaho spoke it then. Today, the Arapaho language is being taught in schools on the Wind River Reservation. The language is still in danger, but now more than 1,000 people speak Arapaho. In 1978, another change occurred that helped the Arapaho. The U.S. government passed a law restoring the rights of native peoples to practice their traditional religions.

40

In 2001, Arapaho and Cheyenne peoples honored their shared past. They succeeded in having the Sand Creek Massacre Site added to the U.S. Register of Historic Places. Ben Nighthorse Campbell, who served in the U.S. Senate from Colorado, is also a Cheyenne chief. He said he was "proud" to have been a major part of this effort.

A dancer performs at a Wyoming powwow.

At powwows, Arapaho people continue to come together to celebrate their traditions. Some Arapaho take part in traditional religious ceremonies as well as Christian ones. The Arapaho are working for a future that includes their traditional values and ways as well as modern conveniences for their people.

41

GLOSSARY

ally—a person or country that helps another person or country

breechcloths—short clothes that wrap around the lower part of someone's body

constitutional—having to do with a constitution, which is a document stating the basic rules of a government

diplomat—a person who is skilled in helping others reach agreements peacefully

immunity—the ability of the body to resist a disease

massacred—killed a large group of unarmed or peaceful people

nomads—people who travel from place to place to hunt and gather food

sinews—strings of tough animal flesh

sweat lodge—building in which heat causes the occupants to perspire to purify the body and spirit

travois—a land sled pulled by animals or people and used to carry things

truce—an agreement between enemies to stop fighting temporarily

DID YOU KNOW?

- Some Arapaho ancestors who moved west went to northern Montana and remained separated from the other Arapaho. They became the Gros Ventre tribe.

- Before the Arapaho had horses, they used a dog to pull each travois. When the Arapaho first saw horses, they called them "star dogs" and "mystery dogs."

- The pink stone called pipestone that the Arapaho and other Plains Indians used to make their sacred pipes is also known as catlinite. This name comes from George Catlin, the 19th-century traveler and artist who wrote about these pipes.

- Several novels and the movie "Soldier Blue" tell the terrible story of the Sand Creek Massacre.

- One way boys and girls on the Wind River Reservation learn to speak Arapaho is by watching the cartoon "Bambi" in Arapaho. Community leaders, Wyoming officials, and the Walt Disney Company worked together to create this version of the classic feature-length cartoon.

Important Dates

Timeline

1600s	Arapaho ancestors start moving west.
1730	Arapaho get horses through trade or raids.
1851	Arapaho and Cheyenne sign a treaty with the U.S government, which the United States breaks.
1864	Cheyenne and Arapaho are massacred at Sand Creek, Colorado.
1869	Southern Arapaho move to Oklahoma with the Southern Cheyenne.
1878	Northern Arapaho settle on the Wind River Reservation with the Shoshone.
1887	Dawes General Allotment Act reduces the size of the southern Arapaho reservation.
1935	Southern Arapaho form a constitutional government with the Cheyenne.
1947	Northern Arapaho tribal leaders gain control of mineral rights on the reservation.
2001	Sand Creek Massacre Site is added to the U.S. Register of Historic Places.

IMPORTANT PEOPLE

CHIEF BLACK COAL (?–1893)

Northern Arapaho leader who traveled to Washington, D.C., to secure a reservation in Wyoming for his people

CHIEF BLACK KETTLE (1800?–1868)

Cheyenne leader who worked for peace but whose people were massacred at Sand Creek; he was killed during another attack by U.S. soldiers four years after the Sand Creek Massacre

COLONEL JOHN M. CHIVINGTON (1821–1894)

Methodist minister who led the U.S. forces that massacred Cheyenne and Arapaho people at Sand Creek in 1864; he was called the "butcher of Sand Creek" but never charged with a crime

PRESIDENT RUTHERFORD B. HAYES (1822–1893)

President who met with Chiefs Black Coal and Sharp Nose and who granted their request for a shared Wyoming reservation with the Shoshone people

CHIEF LITTLE RAVEN (1820?–1889)

Arapaho leader who helped his people keep northern territory in the Wyoming reservation; he also led his people during their first years on this reservation

WANT TO KNOW MORE?

At the Library

Cooper, Michael L. *Indian School: Teaching the White Man's Way.* New York: Clarion Books, 1999.

Gibson, Karen Bush. *The Arapaho: Hunters of the Great Plains.* Mankato, Minn.: Capstone Press, 2003.

Korman, Susan. *Horse Raid: An Arapaho Camp in the 1800s.* Washington, D.C.: Smithsonian Institution, 1998.

Taylor, C. J. *The Ghost and the Lone Warrior: An Arapaho Legend.* Plattsburgh, N.Y.: Tundra Books, 1991.

Turtle, Eagle Walking (Gary McLain). *Full Moon: Thirteen Native American Legends.* New York: Hyperion, 1997.

Wood-Trost, Lucille. *Native Americans of the Plains.* San Diego: Lucent Books, 2000.

On the Web

For more information on the *Arapaho*, use FactHound to track down Web sites related to this book.

1. Go to *www.facthound.com*
2. Type in a search word related to this book or this book ID: 0756508312.
3. Click on the *Fetch It* button.

Your trusty FactHound will fetch the best Web sites for you!

On the Road

St. Michael's Mission and Northern Arapaho Cultural Museum

Wind River Indian Reservation
Ethete, WY 82520
800/244-9106
To see a collection of traditional tools, clothing, and historic photos

The Southern Plains Indian Museum

715 E. Central Blvd.
Andsarko, OK 73005
405/247-6221
To see historic arts and crafts made today by Southern Arapaho and other native peoples

Look for more We the People books about this era:

The Alamo

The Battle of the Little Bighorn

The Buffalo Soldiers

The California Gold Rush

The Chumash and Their History

The Creek and Their History

The Erie Canal

Great Women of the Old West

The Lewis and Clark Expedition

The Louisiana Purchase

The Mexican War

The Ojibwe and Their History

The Oregon Trail

The Pony Express

The Powhatan and Their History

The Santa Fe Trail

The Transcontinental Railroad

The Trail of Tears

The Wampanoag and Their History

The War of 1812

A complete list of We the People titles is available on our Web site:
www.compasspointbooks.com

INDEX

Algonquian languages, 8

Black Coal (chief), 32-33
Black Kettle (Cheyenne chief), 4-5, 7
buffalo, 13-14, 16, 19, 29, 31
business council, 38-39

Carlisle Industrial School, 34-35
ceremonies, 20, 21, 22-24, 37, 41
Cheyenne Indians, 4-5, 6-7, 9, 11, 31, 38, 40
chiefs, 4-5, 6-7, 26-27, 29, 31, 32-33, 36, 41
children, 5-6, 7, 18, 19, 20, 25, 33 34
Chivington, John M., 5, 7
Clark, William, 28-29
clothing, 13, 16, 17
Comanche Indians, 9
"counting coup," 27

Dawes General Allotment Act, 36
diseases, 29

families, 18, 20, 33
food, 12, 13, 16, 20, 21

games, 19
gathering, 16
Ghost Dance movement, 36

gold, 29
Great Plains, 8, 10, 11, 12, 14, 21, 27, 28, 31

horses, 14-15, 27
hunting, 12-13, 15, 19, 20-21

languages, 8, 10, 40
Lewis, Meriwether, 28-29
Little Raven (chief), 31, 36
lodges, 20, 23-24
Louisiana Purchase, 28

marriage, 18
medicine bags, 24-25
medicine men, 24
men, 5, 7, 14-15, 17, 20, 21
mining, 29, 30, 38

nomads, 12, 20-21
Northern Arapaho, 10-11, 30, 32, 33, 38, 39, 40
pain ceremonies, 23
parfleches (hide sacks), 16
Pawnee Indians, 9
Pawnee language, 10
pemmican (food), 16
peyote (plant), 37
population, 10-11

religion, 23-25, 36-37, 40, 41
reservations, 10-11, 31, 33, 36, 38-39, 40

sacred pole, 22, 23
Sand Creek Massacre, 5-7, 31
schools, 34-36
settlers, 10, 14, 27, 29, 31
Sharp Nose (chief), 32-33
Shoshone Indians, 9, 33
sign language, 10
Southern Arapaho, 11, 30, 31, 36, 38
storytelling, 19
sweat lodges, 22

tattoos, 10
tipis (homes), 16-17, 18
tools, 13, 16
trading, 10, 15, 21, 29
travois (transportation device), 15
treaties, 7, 30, 31, 32, 36

Ute Indians, 9
White Antelope (Cheyenne chief), 5, 6-7
Wind River Reservation, 10-11, 40
women, 5, 6, 16, 17, 18, 20

About the Author

Natalie M. Rosinsky writes about history, social studies, economics, science, and other fun things. One of her two cats usually sits on her computer as she works in Mankato, Minnesota. Natalie earned graduate degrees from the University of Wisconsin and has been a high school and college teacher.